LOOSE PIECES

Make Very Special Families

BY: DAWN HICKOK FORBES

tate publishing
CHILDREN'S DIVISION

Published by Tate Publishing & Enterprises, LLC
127 E. Trade Center Terrace | Mustang, Oklahoma 73064 USA
1.888.361.9473 | www.tatepublishing.com

Tate Publishing is committed to excellence in the publishing industry. The company reflects the philosophy established by the founders, based on Psalm 68:11,
"The Lord gave the word and great was the company of those who published it."

Book design copyright © 2015 by Tate Publishing, LLC. All rights reserved.
Cover and interior design by Rhezette Fiel

Published in the United States of America

ISBN: 978-1-68028-615-1
1. Juvenile Nonfiction / Family / Adoption
2. Juvenile Nonfiction / Poetry / General
14.11.25

A BOOK ABOUT
ADOPTION THE PLAN OF GOD

Long ago—before there was time

In the mind of God He had a design

For there to be families—some sisters,
some brothers

So they could take care of and love one another.

For you created my inmost being; you knit me together in my mother's womb. Your eyes saw my unformed body. All the days ordained for me were written in your book before one of them came to be.

—Psalm 139:13 and 16 (NIV)

He gave mommies soft hearts that need
little children

And daddies strong arms to love and support them.

And that was the way He planned it to be—

In the mind of God—In eternity.

From heaven the Lord looks down and sees all mankind; He
who forms the hearts of all, who considers everything they
do. In him our hearts rejoice, for we trust in his holy name.

—Psalm 33:13, 15, 21 (NIV)

But the world became evil

And things weren't so good

And the families didn't always behave as
they should.

Some children were left without daddies
and mommies

Some without homes—no food in their tummies.

This is what the Lord says: "Stand at the crossroads and look;
ask for the ancient paths, ask where the good way is and walk
in it." But you said, "We will not walk in it."

—Jeremiah 6:16 (NIV)

For everything in the world—the cravings of sinful man, the
lust of his eyes and the boasting of what he has and does—
comes not from the Father but from the world.

—1 John 2:16 (NIV)

And what is a home with no children to play.

Mommy's arms empty day after day.

And hearts sad and broken—no joy of their own,

Without being able to bring babies home.

Who is like the Lord our God, the one who sits enthroned on high, who stoops down to look on the heavens and the earth? He settles the barren woman in her home as a happy mother of children.

—Psalm 113:5, 6, 9 (NIV)

So God in His goodness looked down on such sorrow

And spoke to His children—"There's hope
for tomorrow.

Remember, my children, when I sent my son

And He gave His own life that we might be one."

A rainbow of children, no color was odd,

Adopted together—the family of God.

In love he predestined us to be adopted as his sons through
Jesus Christ, in accordance with his pleasure and will—to the
praise of his glorious grace, which he has freely given us in the
One he loves. In him we have redemption through his blood,
the forgiveness of sins.

—Ephesians 1:4b–5 (NIV)

The pattern was done, and by His great plan,

He'll fill empty homes of women and men

And placing those children with no one to love,

He gives guidance and patience, which comes
from above.

Love the Lord with all your heart and with all your soul and
with all your strength. These commandments that I give
you today are to be upon your hearts. Impress them on your
children. Talk about them when you sit at home and when
you walk along the road, when you lie down and when you
get up.

—Deuteronomy 6:5–7 (NIV)

He takes up loose pieces, not quite like all others,

And turns the sad hearts into Fathers and Mothers

A family is born—such was His decree,

In the mind of God—in eternity.

Praise him who rides on the clouds—his name is the Lord—and rejoice before him. A father to the fatherless, a defender of widows, is God in his holy dwelling. God sets the lonely in families.

—Psalm 68:4b–6 (NIV)

e|LIVE

listen|imagine|view|experience

AUDIO BOOK DOWNLOAD INCLUDED WITH THIS BOOK!

In your hands you hold a complete digital entertainment package. In addition to the paper version, you receive a free download of the audio version of this book. Simply use the code listed below when visiting our website. Once downloaded to your computer, you can listen to the book through your computer's speakers, burn it to an audio CD or save the file to your portable music device (such as Apple's popular iPod) and listen on the go!

How to get your free audio book digital download:

1. Visit www.tatepublishing.com and click on the e|LIVE logo on the home page.
2. Enter the following coupon code:
   611b-a5ef-155b-93d1-cc99-0c1e-3dfe-be03
3. Download the audio book from your e|LIVE digital locker and begin enjoying your new digital entertainment package today!